#JUST GETTING STARTED

OR

#STARTING OVER

PART TWO

BASIC INVESTING

BY

FRUGAL FRANNIE P

©2025

ALL RIGHTS RESERVED

Whether you are just starting out or starting over, I hope that this book helps you move one step a day towards your financial freedom journey.

*DISCLAIMER: I AM NOT A PROFESSIONAL. THIS IS FOR EDUCATIONAL/INFORMATIONAL PURPOSES ONLY. THIS IS A SIMPLE BASIC GUIDE TO GETTING STARTED OR STARTING OVER.
INVEST AT YOUR OWN RISK.

"Investing is like planting seeds. You put a tiny seed in the dirt, and after some time, it grows into a big tree with lots of fruit. The longer you wait, the bigger the tree gets and the more fruit it gives you."

So, investing means putting your money somewhere safe and letting it grow over time, just like the seed grows into a tree.

Welcome to your first step

towards your

financial freedom journey!!

This book belongs

to:

____

TABLE OF CONTENTS

The path to financial freedom is like a fun adventure where you learn how to make, save, and use your money wisely so you can do the things you love without worrying. Here's how it works, step by step:

Earn Money: First, you need to earn money by doing chores, helping others, or working when you're older. It's like collecting treasure on your journey!

Save Money: Put some of your money in a piggy bank or savings jar. This helps you save for bigger things you want, like a special toy. Saving is like storing snacks for later when you get hungry!

Spend Wisely: Only spend money on things you really need or love. It's like choosing your favorite candy at the store instead of buying everything.

Avoid Too Much Debt: Don't borrow too much money from others because you'll have to pay it back. It's like borrowing your friend's toy—you need to return it, so you can't keep borrowing all the time.

Invest Money: When you grow up, you can put money into things that grow bigger over time, like planting seeds that turn into a money tree.

Keep Learning: Keep learning about money so you can make smart choices. It's like getting better at your favorite game by practicing.

Financial freedom means you have enough money saved and growing so you can do fun things, take care of yourself, and not worry too much about the cost. It's like having a magic key that opens doors to your dreams!

NOTES

TOPIC ______________________ DATE ______________

NOTES

ACTION ITEMS

- [ ]
- [ ]
- [ ]
- [ ]
- [ ]

GETTING INSURANCE

Getting insurance is like having a big safety net to protect you and your family. It helps you feel safe if something bad happens.

For example:

For your family: Life insurance gives your family money to buy food, clothes, or toys if you can't be there to help them.

For your stuff: Car insurance or house insurance helps fix things if they get broken. Some people get insurance on their cellphones, televisions, tablets, computers, and washing machines in case they get broken.

For your health: Health insurance helps pay the doctor when you're sick.

Insurance is there to help when things go wrong, so you don't have to worry too much!

THE DIFFICULT CONVERSATION

You probably own a cellphone worth at least $500-$1,000+ and have insurance on it, in case you need to get it fixed, or replaced. You make monthly insurance payments in case of something happening to it. You have placed a value on your cellphone.

What about you?

What type of value would you place on yourself in the event that something would happen to you?

What about your family?

How could you help your family even if you are no longer here to help them?

I know this is a difficult conversation to think about, but it is necessary.

BASIC INVESTMENT #1
INVEST IN YOURSELF AND GET LIFE INSURANCE

Life Insurance offers some protection and peace of mind for you and your loved ones. It provides financial security for your family in the event of you or someone in your family's untimely passing. The benefit can help cover funeral and burial costs, living expenses, outstanding debts, and future financial needs, ensuring that your loved ones maintain their quality of life even in you
or someone in your family's absence.

WHAT IS LIFE INSURANCE?

Life insurance is like a promise you make to take care of your family, even if you're not there. You pay a little money every month, and if something happens to you, the insurance company gives your family money to help them buy things they need, like food, clothes, or a house. It's a way to show you love them and want them to be safe!

Life insurance is like a big hug for your family if something bad happens. It's a way to make sure they have money to take care of important things, like buying food, paying for a house, or going to school, even if you're not there to help. It's a way to show you love them and want them to be okay, no matter what.

Life insurance is important because it helps take care of your family if something happens to you. It's like leaving a big present of money to help them buy food, pay for their home, and stay safe. It's a way to make sure your family is okay, even if you can't be there to help them yourself. It shows how much you love them!

TO-DO LIST

#1	
#2	
#3	
#4	
#5	

TO-DO LIST

#6	
#7	
#8	
#9	
#10	

NOTES

TOPIC ______________________ **DATE** ______________

NOTES

ACTION ITEMS

- [ ]
- [ ]
- [ ]
- [ ]
- [ ]

Why Do You Need Life Insurance?

Life insurance is a critical component of a comprehensive financial plan, offering protection and peace of mind for you and your loved ones. Here are several compelling reasons why life insurance having is important:

1. Financial Security for Loved Ones

Life insurance provides financial security for your family in the event of your untimely death. The death benefit can help cover living expenses, outstanding debts, and future financial needs, ensuring that your loved ones maintain their quality of life even in your absence.

2. Debt Repayment

Many people have significant debts, such as mortgages, car loans, or credit card balances. Life insurance can help pay off these debts, preventing your family from being burdened with financial obligations that they may struggle to meet without your income.

3. Income Replacement

For families that rely on your income, life insurance acts as a vital income replacement. The payout can help replace lost earnings, allowing your family to cover daily expenses, maintain their lifestyle, and fulfill long-term financial goals, such as funding children's education.

4. Funeral and Burial Costs

Funeral and burial expenses can be substantial, often costing thousands of dollars. Life insurance can cover these costs, alleviating the financial strain on your family during a difficult time and allowing them to focus on grieving and healing.

5. Estate Planning

Life insurance can be an essential tool in estate planning, providing liquidity to pay estate taxes and ensuring a smooth transfer of assets to your heirs. This can preserve the value of your estate and prevent the need to sell assets to cover tax liabilities.

6. Business Continuity

For business owners, life insurance can support business continuity by providing funds to cover business debts, buy out a deceased partner's shares, or finance a smooth transition of ownership. This ensures the stability and longevity of your business in the face of unexpected events.

7. Peace of Mind

Having life insurance offers peace of mind, knowing that your loved ones are financially protected if something were to happen to you. This assurance allows you to focus on enjoying life without worrying about the financial impact of unforeseen circumstances.

8. Charitable Contributions

Life insurance can also be used to leave a legacy by designating a portion of the death benefit to a charitable organization. This allows you to support causes that are important to you, even after you're gone.

In conclusion, life insurance is an essential safeguard that provides financial protection and peace of mind. It ensures that your loved ones are cared for, your debts are paid, and your financial legacy is preserved, making it a crucial part of any sound financial plan.

TO-DO LIST

#1	
#2	
#3	
#4	
#5	

TO-DO LIST

#6	
#7	
#8	
#9	
#10	

NOTES

TOPIC ______________________ DATE ______________

NOTES

ACTION ITEMS

- [ ]
- [ ]
- [ ]
- [ ]
- [ ]

WHOLE LIFE AND TERM LIFE

Whole life insurance and term insurance are like two kinds of piggy banks for your family:

Whole life insurance is like a piggy bank that lasts forever. You put money in, and it grows over time. If something happens to you, your family gets the money. Even if you get very old, the money will still be there.

Term insurance is like a piggy bank that works for a certain time, like 10 or 20 years. If something happens to you during that time, your family gets the money. But after the time is up, it doesn't work anymore.

Both are ways to make sure your family has money to take care of them!

WHOLE LIFE INSURANCE

Whole life insurance is like having a magic piggy bank for your family. You put money into it every month, and it keeps growing and growing. If something happens to you, the piggy bank gives your family money to help them with things like food, a house, or school. And the best part? This piggy bank never goes away, no matter how old you get! It's there to help forever.

Having a whole life insurance policy is like having a magic piggy bank that helps your family in many ways! Here are the advantages:

Lasts Forever: This piggy bank never goes away. It's there for your whole life, no matter how old you get.

Money Grows: As you put money in, it grows bigger, like planting a money tree that keeps growing over time.

Helps Your Family: If something happens to you, the magic piggy bank gives your family money to help with things they need, like food, clothes, and school.

You Can Use It Too: If you need money later, you can take some out of the piggy bank to help you with big things, like buying a car or fixing your house.

It's a special way to take care of your family and yourself!

TO-DO LIST

#1	
#2	
#3	
#4	
#5	

TO-DO LIST

#6	
#7	
#8	
#9	
#10	

NOTES

TOPIC ______________________ DATE ______________

NOTES

ACTION ITEMS

- [ ]
- [ ]
- [ ]
- [ ]
- [ ]

TERM LIFE INSURANCE

Term life insurance is like a piggy bank that works for only a little while, like 10 or 20 years. You put money in every month, and if something happens to you during that time, it gives your family money to help them. But after the time is up, the piggy bank stops working. It's good for when your family needs help for a certain time, like while they're growing up.

Having a term life insurance policy is like having a helpful piggy bank for a little while. Here are the advantages:

Costs Less: It doesn't take as much money to keep this piggy bank working, so it's easier to use.

Helps When Needed Most: It's there to help your family during an important time, like when they're growing up or paying for school

.

Big Help for Your Family: If something happens to you, this piggy bank gives your family money to help with things they need, like food, clothes, or their house.

It's a simple and smart way to make sure your family has what they need for a certain time!

TO-DO LIST

#1	
#2	
#3	
#4	
#5	

TO-DO LIST

#6	
#7	
#8	
#9	
#10	

NOTES

TOPIC ____________________ **DATE** ____________

NOTES

ACTION ITEMS

- [ ]
- [ ]
- [ ]
- [ ]
- [ ]

SAMPLE LIST OF 14

LIFE INSURANCE COMPANIES (EXAMPLE IN NEW YORK)

GERBER LIFE INSURANCE

PRIMERICA

SECURITY MUTUAL LIFE INSURANCE COMPANY OF NEW YORK

MET LIFE

STATE FARM

NEW YORK LIFE

AIG (AMERICAN INTERNATIONAL GROUP)

PRUDENTIAL

FARMER'S INSURANCE

GUARDIAN LIFE

JOHN HANCOCK

MASS MUTUAL (MASSACHUSETTS MUTUAL LIFE INSURANCE COMPANY)

NORTHWESTERN MUTUAL

TRANSAMERICA

When selecting a life insurance policy, it's important to compare options and consult with an agent to find the best coverage for your situation.

Choosing the Right Insurance Company

When looking for life insurance in New York, it's important to:

Compare premiums: See which company offers the best rates for the coverage you need.

Check financial strength: Make sure the company can pay claims. Look for high ratings from agencies like A.M. Best, Moody's, or S&P.

Customer service: Ensure the company has good reviews for customer service and ease of filing claims.

You can contact these companies directly or use a licensed insurance agent to help you choose the best policy for your needs!

REAL ESTATE INVESTMENT ADVICE #1

that I was given but did not act on

On social media, a real estate investor was surprised that an eighteen-year-old male was interested in buying an investment property.

He said he would be back in two days with the downpayment. He asked the teenager if he was rich and the guy replied "no." He said "You are so young. How are you able to have that kind of money? The young man replied, "Well in my family, when you have a baby, the head of the family takes out a whole life insurance policy on the baby when it's two weeks old. The family pays the monthly premiums (which are cheap because the policy was taken out when they were babies) for years, and when the child turns 18, they have the option to take out a loan against the policy. The loan is used as a down payment towards a real estate investment property. This is how my family has been able to invest in real estate properties for each immediate family member using whole life insurance."

NOTES

TOPIC ______________________ **DATE** ______________

NOTES

ACTION ITEMS

WHAT IS INVESTING?

Investing is like planting seeds in a garden so they can grow into big, strong trees with lots of fruit! Here's how it works in a way that's easy to understand:

Start with a little money: Just like planting a small seed, you start with some money you saved.

Put it in a special place: Instead of planting in the dirt, you put your money in places where it can grow, like stocks, bonds, or mutual funds. These are like different gardens where your money can grow bigger over time.

Wait patiently: Just like it takes time for a seed to grow into a tree, it takes time for your money to grow. You can't rush it!

Watch it grow: Over time, your money can grow bigger if you leave it alone. Sometimes it might not grow as much, just like some trees grow faster than others, but if you're patient, it usually gets bigger.

Reap the rewards: After a while, your tree (or your money) will grow big enough to give you fruit! You can use that "fruit" (your extra money) to buy things, save more, or invest again.

Investing is a way to make your money grow so you can have more in the future, like a garden full of yummy fruits!

TO-DO LIST

#1	
#2	
#3	
#4	
#5	

TO-DO LIST

#6	
#7	
#8	
#9	
#10	

NOTES

TOPIC ______________________ DATE ______________

NOTES

ACTION ITEMS

- [ ]
- [ ]
- [ ]
- [ ]
- [ ]

Why Do You Need a Basic Investment Account?

A basic investment account is a crucial financial tool that can play a significant role in building and maintaining your financial health. Here are several reasons why having a basic investment account is important:

1. Wealth Accumulation

A basic investment account allows you to invest in various financial instruments, such as stocks, bonds, and mutual funds, providing the opportunity to grow your wealth over time. By generating returns on your investments, this account can help increase your overall net worth compared to simply saving money.

2. Inflation Hedge

Investing through a basic account can help protect your money from inflation, which erodes purchasing power. Investments typically offer higher returns than traditional savings accounts, allowing your money to grow at a rate that can outpace inflation and maintain its real value over time.

3. Meeting Financial Goals

Whether you are saving for a home, education, retirement, or other long-term goals, a basic investment account can help you reach these objectives more effectively. By strategically allocating your funds, you can build the necessary financial resources to achieve significant life milestones.

4. Diversification

A basic investment account allows you to diversify your portfolio by spreading your investments across different asset classes. Diversification reduces the risk associated with any single investment, enhancing the overall stability and performance of your portfolio.

5. Generating Passive Income

Investments can generate passive income streams, such as dividends from stocks or interest from bonds. This income can supplement your primary earnings, providing additional financial security and flexibility.

6. Preparation for Retirement

Investing is essential for retirement planning. A basic investment account can help you accumulate the necessary funds to sustain your lifestyle once you retire. By consistently contributing to your investments, you can build a substantial nest egg for the future.

7. Financial Literacy and Empowerment

Managing a basic investment account encourages financial literacy and empowers you to make informed decisions about your money. This experience can enhance your understanding of market dynamics, risk management, and financial planning, contributing to your overall financial confidence.

8. Economic Contribution

Investing supports the broader economy by providing capital to businesses and governments. This capital facilitates growth, innovation, and infrastructure development, benefiting society as a whole. By investing, you contribute to economic progress and prosperity.

In conclusion, a basic investment account is an essential tool for building wealth, protecting against inflation, and achieving financial goals. It offers diversification, passive income, and valuable financial insights, making it a cornerstone of a sound financial strategy.

AN EMPLOYEE SPONSORED RETIREMENT PLAN (401K, 403B, 457)

Imagine you have a piggy bank where you save your coins. Now, imagine your mom or dad also puts in extra coins every time you save your own. This makes your piggy bank grow even faster!

An employee-sponsored retirement plan is like that piggy bank, but for grown-ups who are saving money for when they're older and don't want to work anymore. The place they work helps them save by adding extra money into their big piggy bank when they save some of their own.

WHAT IS A 401 K PLAN?

A 401(k) plan is like a special piggy bank for when you grow up and stop working. Here's how it works:

Saving Money for Later: Imagine you have a big adventure coming when you're older, like building your dream castle. A 401(k) is a piggy bank where you save money to help pay for that adventure.

Work Gives You Money: When you have a job, your boss helps you put some of the money you earn into this piggy bank. It's like your boss giving you extra coins to save.

Money Grows: The money in the 401(k) doesn't just sit there. It grows bigger over time, like magic beans turning into a big beanstalk. This happens because it's invested in things that grow, like companies or projects.

Wait Until You're Older: You don't take the money out of this piggy bank right away. You have to wait until you're older–like a grown-up ready to enjoy a big treasure hunt.

Special Bonus: Sometimes, your boss adds extra money to your piggy bank to help it grow faster. That's called a "match," like finding extra treasure!

A 401(k) is a smart way to save for your future adventures and make sure you have enough money to live happily when you're older.

ADVANTAGES OF HAVING A 401 K PLAN

A 401(k) plan is like a grown-up's treasure chest for saving money! Here's why it's super cool:

Free Extra Money: Sometimes, the grown-up's boss puts extra money into the treasure chest to help them save more. It's like getting bonus candies just for saving yours!

Money Grows Bigger: The money in the chest grows over time, like a plant that gets bigger and bigger if you water it. Grown-ups don't have to do much - it just grows!

Save Before Spending: Grown-ups put money in the chest before they have to pay for things like taxes. This means they can save more money faster.

For the Future: The treasure chest is locked until they're older and stop working. Then they can use the money to buy food, clothes, or even go on fun trips when they don't have a job anymore.

It's a smart way for grown-ups to save up for a happy life later, just like saving your favorite toys or candies for a special day!

WHAT IS A 403B PLAN?

A 403(b) plan is like a special piggy bank for people who work at schools, hospitals, or other places that help people, so they can save money for when they grow up and stop working. Here's how it works:

Saving for the Future: Imagine you're saving for something big when you're older, like a trip to the moon! A 403(b) is a piggy bank where people can put their money to save for when they're older.

Work Gives You Money to Save: When someone works at a school or hospital, they can take a little bit of the money they earn and put it in this special piggy bank. It's like saving candy from Halloween to enjoy later!

Money Grows Like Magic: The money in the 403(b) doesn't just stay the same. It grows bigger over time because it's invested in things that grow, like a magical garden.

Don't Open It Too Soon: The 403(b) piggy bank has a rule: you have to wait until you're older—like a grown-up—before you can take the money out. That's to make sure it's saved for when you really need it.

Special Bonus Sometimes: Sometimes, the boss might add extra money to the piggy bank, like a surprise gift, to help it grow even faster.

A 403(b) plan is a smart way for people who work in special jobs to save money for their future adventures!

ADVANTAGES OF HAVING A 403 B PLAN

A 403(b) plan is like a special piggy bank for grown-ups who work at places like schools, hospitals, or charities. Here's why it's super helpful:

Grows Like Magic: The money in the piggy bank grows bigger over time, like planting a seed and watching it grow into a big tree with lots of fruit!

Boss Helps Sometimes: Sometimes, the grown-up's boss puts extra money into the piggy bank to help them save more. It's like when a friend shares extra candies with you.

Save More, Faster: Grown-ups get to put money in the piggy bank before they pay for things like taxes, so they can save more quickly.

For Later: The piggy bank stays closed until they're older and not working anymore. Then they can use the money to buy the things they need, like food or a comfy place to live.

It's like a smart way to save for the future, just like you might save your favorite toy to play with on a special day!

WHAT IS A 457 PLAN?

A 457 plan is like a piggy bank that grown-ups use to save money for when they stop working someday. They put some of their money into this special piggy bank, and it stays safe and grows over time. When they're older and don't work anymore, they can open the piggy bank and use the money to buy things they need. It's like saving your favorite toys in a box for later, so you have something special when you need it!

A 457 plan is like a super special piggy bank for grown-ups who have jobs like being teachers, firefighters, or other helpers. They put money in this piggy bank to save for when they're older and don't work anymore.

The cool part? The money in the piggy bank grows bigger all by itself, like magic! And when the grown-ups are ready to stop working, they can open the piggy bank and use the money to buy what they need. It helps them feel safe and happy when they're older!

ADVANTAGES OF HAVING A 457 PLAN

Imagine you have a big jar where you can save your favorite candies. A 457 plan is like that jar, but for grown-ups saving money. Here's why it's awesome:

Grows Bigger Over Time: It's like putting a magic candy in your jar that grows into more candies while you wait. The money grows while it's saved.

Special Savings Rules: Grown-ups don't have to share some of their money with the tax people right away when they put it in the jar, so they can save more!

Use It When Needed: When they get older and stop working, they can open the jar and use the money to buy important things, like food and clothes, or to have fun!

Extra Safe Spot: It's a safe place to keep their money so they don't spend it all at once, just like your candy jar keeps your sweets safe for later!

So, it's like a super-smart way for grown-ups to save up for their future, just like you save your candies for a special day.

NOTES

TOPIC ______________________ **DATE** ______________

NOTES

ACTION ITEMS

- [ ]
- [ ]
- [ ]
- [ ]
- [ ]

TO-DO LIST

#1	
#2	
#3	
#4	
#5	

TO-DO LIST

#6	
#7	
#8	
#9	
#10	

NOTES

TOPIC ______________________ **DATE** ____________

NOTES

ACTION ITEMS

- [ ]
- [ ]
- [ ]
- [ ]
- [ ]

WHAT IS AN IRA?
INDIVIDUAL RETIREMENT ACCOUNT

An IRA is like a special piggy bank that grown-ups use to save money for when they're older and stop working. Here's how it works in simple terms:

Save for the Future: Imagine you're saving for a big adventure, like building your dream castle. An IRA is a piggy bank where grown-ups save money so they can have enough when they're old and not working anymore.

Money Grows: The money in the IRA doesn't just sit there—it grows bigger over time because it's invested in things like companies or projects. It's like planting seeds that grow into money trees!

Two Kinds of IRAs:

Traditional IRA: You don't pay taxes when you put the money in, but you pay taxes later when you take it out. It's like saving candy now but giving one piece back when you eat it later.

Roth IRA: You pay taxes now when you put the money in, but later, you can take it out tax-free. It's like buying candy today and keeping it all for yourself later!

Wait Until You're Older: You have to wait until you're a grown-up (59 ½ years old) to take the money out, so you don't run out of savings too early.

An IRA is a smart way for grown-ups to save money, let it grow, and make sure they have enough for their future adventures!

WHAT IS A TRADITIONAL IRA?

A Traditional IRA is like a piggy bank that helps grown-ups save money for when they get older and stop working. Here's how it works in a fun way:

Put Money In: Grown-ups take some of the money they earn and put it in this special piggy bank to save for the future. It's like putting your favorite candy aside for later.

No Taxes Now: When they put money in, they don't have to pay taxes on it right away. It's like getting to keep all your candy without sharing any for now.

Money Grows: The money in the piggy bank grows over time because it's invested in things like companies or projects. It's like planting candy seeds that grow into a candy tree!

Pay Taxes Later: When grown-ups are older and take the money out of the piggy bank, they have to pay taxes on it then. It's like saving your candy now but sharing a little bit when you eat it later.

Wait Until You're Older: You can't take the money out until you're a grown-up (59 ½ years old) without paying a penalty. This makes sure the piggy bank is saved for when you really need it.

A Traditional IRA is a smart way for grown-ups to save money, let it grow, and get ready for their big dreams when they're older!

WHAT IS A ROTH IRA?

A Roth IRA is like a super cool piggy bank that helps grown-ups save money for when they're older, with some special magic. Here's how it works:

Put In Money You've Already Paid Taxes On: Imagine you have some shiny coins from your allowance. You put those coins into the Roth IRA piggy bank after paying for the things you need, like your candy tax.

Money Grows Over Time: The coins in this piggy bank are special—they grow bigger over time, like planting magic seeds that turn into a money tree.

No Taxes Later: When you grow up and want to take the money out, you don't have to pay any taxes on it. It's like having candy that stays all yours, with no sharing when you finally eat it.

Wait Until You're Older: You have to wait until you're a grown-up (59 ½ years old) to take the money out, so it stays safe for something important, like a big adventure or a comfy house.

Use for Special Things: If you need it earlier for something important, like going to school or buying your first home, you can take out some money without any problems.

A Roth IRA is a magical piggy bank that helps grown-ups save money, let it grow, and keep it safe for their future dreams!

What is a SEP-IRA?

A SEP-IRA is like a special piggy bank for grown-ups who are their own boss or have a very small business. Here's how it works, in a way that's fun for a four-year-old:

For Grown-Ups Who Work for Themselves: Imagine you're the captain of your own ship, and you want to save treasure for when you're older. A SEP-IRA is a piggy bank made just for people like ship captains who run their own crew.

Put In a Lot of Money: This piggy bank is bigger than a regular one, so grown-ups can put in more money each year. It's like having a giant treasure chest instead of a small jar.

Money Grows Over Time: The money in the SEP-IRA grows bigger, like magic beans turning into a beanstalk. It gets bigger because it's invested in things that grow, like companies or projects.

Wait Until You're Older: Just like other special piggy banks, you can't take the money out until you're a grown-up (59 ½ years old), so it's saved for important things in the future.

Good for the Captain and the Crew: If the captain (the boss) has a crew (employees), they can also help their crew save money by putting treasure in SEP-IRAs for them too.

A SEP-IRA is a smart way for grown-ups who are in charge of their own work to save lots of money and let it grow for the future!

TO-DO LIST

#1	
#2	
#3	
#4	
#5	

TO-DO LIST

#6	
#7	
#8	
#9	
#10	

NOTES

TOPIC ______________________ DATE ______________

NOTES

ACTION ITEMS

- [ ]
- [ ]
- [ ]
- [ ]
- [ ]

BASIC INVESTMENTS

1. Stocks

Stocks are like owning a tiny piece of a big company.

Imagine you and your friends all share a big pizza. If you buy one slice, you own a part of the pizza. That's like owning stock in a company—you own a small piece of it.

2. Bonds

Bonds are like lending money to someone and getting it back with extra.

If you let a friend borrow your toy and they give it back with a sticker as a thank-you, that's like a bond. You let someone borrow your money, and they pay you back with a little extra.

3. Mutual Funds

Mutual funds are like everyone pitching in to buy a variety of toys.

You and your friends put your money together to buy a big toy box with lots of different toys inside. A mutual fund is a way people pool their money to buy many different stocks or bonds together.

BASIC SIMPLE INVESTMENT ADVICE #2 that I heard but I didn't act on.

Many years ago, I remember watching a tv show, and a lady in the audience was in her twenties and she was a millionaire. When asked, how did she become a millionaire, she said that she invested in stocks. She looked around her entire home and made a list of the things she and her family purchased on a regular basis, and did her research to see if the products were on the stock market. Then she invested and reinvested in the companies and she became a millionaire over time. She made a list of products that her family uses on a regular basis like soap, toothpaste, mouthwash, toilet tissue, paper napkins, feminine products, detergent, and cleaning supplies.

Then she made a list of things that she personally doesn't use, but other people use on a regular basis, like baby food, pampers, wipes, baby clothes, baby products, toys, games, and she invested in those companies as well.

Then she made a list of things that she might be interested in the future, that other people are currently buying, like brand name and designer items, clothes, accessories, luxury cars, retail stores, and electronics, etc.

The young lady in the audience was not flashy, as a matter of fact, she was quite plain, compared to the other audience members. But they were totally shocked when they learned that she was a millionaire!

I'm not saying that this is a guarantee to become rich.

INVEST AT YOUR OWN RISK.

A PUBLICLY TRADED COMPANY

Imagine a really big toy store that lots of people love. This toy store is so big that it doesn't just belong to one person–it's like a giant puzzle, and each piece of the puzzle is owned by someone. These pieces are called "shares."

When a company is "publicly traded," it means anyone can buy a piece of the puzzle (a share) and own a tiny bit of the toy store. If the store does really well and sells lots of toys, the pieces of the puzzle can become more valuable. So, owning a piece means you get to share in the store's success!

ASSIGNMENT #1

- TAKE YOUR TIME AND LOOK AT EACH ITEM IN EACH ROOM.
- LOOK AT PRODUCTS YOU BUY REGULARLY, AND PRODUCTS YOU BUY ONCE IN A WHILE.
- LOOK AT PRODUCTS THAT YOU BOUGHT EVEN ONCE.
- EACH PRODUCT ON THE BACK OR THE SIDE OR THE BOTTOM, SHOULD HAVE A LABEL WITH A BRAND NAME AND/OR A COMPANY NAME AND WHERE IT'S MADE.
- MAKE A LIST OF THE DIFFERENT PRODUCTS AND COMPANIES.
- CHECK TO SEE IF THEY ARE ON THE STOCK MARKET AND WHAT THE CURRENT PRICE IS FOR THAT STOCK

.

- FOR EXAMPLE: SCOTT TISSUE (TOILET PAPER) IS OWNED BY THE KIMBERLY CLARK COMPANY IN PHILADELPHIA PENNSYLVANIA SINCE 1879. THEY MAKE TOILET PAPER AND PAPER TOWELS. KIMBERLY-CLARK CORP STOCK IS SOLD ON THE NYSE (NEW YORK STOCK EXCHANGE) AND THE SYMBOL IS KMB THE CURRENT STOCK PRICE IS $125.43

INVEST AT YOUR OWN RISK- THIS IS NOT A GUARANTEE.

MAKE A LIST OF PRODUCTS AND COMPANIES AROUND YOUR HOME

CHECK TO SEE IF THEY ARE PUBLIC COMPANIES ON THE STOCK MARKET

SCOTT TISSUE	JOHNSON AND JOHNSON	PROCTOR AND GAMBLE	PFIZER	MODERNA	ENERGIZER	UNICHARM
CLOROX	HUGGIES	ALWAYS MAXI PADS	FEBREZE	DURACELL	STAYFREE PADS	ESSITY
COCA-COLA	PEPSI-COLA	TAMPAX	SONY	DISNEY	STARZ	YOUTUBE
FILA	CONVERSE	HANES	OPTIMUM			
APPLE	DELL	HEWLETT PACKARD	MICROSOFT	GOOGLE ALPHABET	FACEBOOK META PLATFORMS	LENOVO

YAHOO	UPS	FEDEX	USPS	DHL	AMAZON	TIKTOK
MCDONALDS	BURGER KING	WHITE CASTLE	POPRYRD	DOMINOES	PAPA JOHNS	KFC
CON EDISON	SPECTRUM	VERIZON	FIOS	T-MOBILE	GAP	CHIOPTLE
RALPH LAUREN	GUCCI	LOUIS VUITTON	COACH	COSTCO	ALDI	TRADER JOES
NIKE	ADIDAS	PUMA	SKECHERS	MACYS	BURLINGTON	MARSHALLS

BATHROOM PRODUCTS

#1	
#2	
#3	
#4	
#5	

BATHROOM PRODUCTS

#6	
#7	
#8	
#9	
#10	

KITCHEN PRODUCTS

#1	
#2	
#3	
#4	
#5	

KITCHEN PRODUCTS

#6	
#7	
#8	
#9	
#10	

LIVING ROOM PRODUCTS

#1	
#2	
#3	
#4	
#5	

LIVING ROOM PRODUCTS

#6	
#7	
#8	
#9	
#10	

BEDROOM PRODUCTS

#1	
#2	
#3	
#4	
#5	

BEDROOM PRODUCTS

#6	
#7	
#8	
#9	
#10	

STOCKS

1. Ownership and Growth Potential

Buying stocks means owning a piece of a company, which can offer significant growth potential. As the company succeeds and its value increases, so does the value of your shares, potentially leading to substantial capital gains.

2. Dividend Income

Many stocks pay dividends, providing a regular income stream. This can be particularly attractive for investors seeking both growth and income.

3. Liquidity

Stocks are typically more liquid than other investment options, meaning they can be bought and sold relatively quickly, providing flexibility in managing your portfolio.

TYPES OF STOCKS

Stocks are like owning little pieces of a company, and there are different types of stocks that work in different ways.

1. Common Stocks

What it is: If you buy common stock, you own a small piece of a company and get to vote on big decisions.

Example: Imagine you and your friends build a lemonade stand. If you own common stock, you get a say in what flavor to make next and earn a little money if the stand makes a profit.

2. Preferred Stocks

What it is: Preferred stock means you don't get to vote on company decisions, but you're first in line to get money if the company earns profits.

Example: It's like being the first person to pick a cupcake from the tray.

This is like getting a special VIP ticket to the company party. You don't get to vote on the games, but you always get the first candy (money) before anyone else if the company does well. It's great if you like to know you'll get candy first.

3. Growth Stocks

These stocks are like planting a tiny seed that grows into a big tree over time. The company doesn't share candy (money) right away because it's using all its energy to grow bigger and stronger.

4. Dividend Stocks

These are like candy-sharing stocks.

The company gives you a little candy (money) regularly, even if it's not growing very fast. It's like getting a small treat every week.

5. Blue-Chip Stocks

These are like the superstars of the stock world—companies everyone knows and trusts, like your favorite superhero.

They're big and steady, so people feel safe owning their stocks.

6. Penny Stocks

These are like tiny, inexpensive toys that might grow into something big, but they're risky because they can break easily.

People hope they'll turn into something valuable, but it doesn't always happen.

7. Defensive Stocks

These are like having an umbrella on a rainy day.

Even when the weather is bad (the economy is slow), these stocks stay strong because the company makes things people always need, like food or medicine.

8. Cyclical Stocks

These stocks are like ice cream in summer—people want them when things are good, but not as much when it's cold or tough outside.

The company's value can go up and down a lot, like the seasons.

Stocks are just like tickets to be part of different kinds of companies, and each type works a little differently!

PICKING A STOCK

Picking a stock can be like choosing your favorite toy or snack! Let me explain how you can start by looking around your house:

Find What You Love: Look at things you use every day. Maybe it's the TV you watch, the cereal you eat, or the shoes you wear. Grown-ups call these "brands" or "companies."

Ask Questions: Think about which ones you really like. If your cereal makes you happy every morning, or if your favorite shoes keep your feet comfy, those might be good companies to learn about.

Learn About the Company: Grown-ups can find out if the company is doing well–like checking if it's making money and if lots of other people like their things too.

Imagine the Future: Think about if the company will keep making good things for a long time. If it's something people will always need or love, it might be a good one to pick.

So, it's like choosing your favorite snack because you know it's tasty, and you think other kids will want it too!

TO-DO LIST

#1	
#2	
#3	
#4	
#5	

TO-DO LIST

#6	
#7	
#8	
#9	
#10	

NOTES

TOPIC ____________________ DATE __________

NOTES

ACTION ITEMS

- [ ]
- [ ]
- [ ]
- [ ]
- [ ]

BONDS

4. Stability and Predictable Income

Bonds offer more stability compared to stocks, as they provide fixed interest payments over time. This predictable income can help balance the volatility of stock investments.

5. Capital Preservation

Bonds are generally considered less risky than stocks, making them a good choice for preserving capital, especially for conservative investors or those nearing retirement.

6. Diversification

Including bonds in your portfolio can help diversify your investments, reducing overall risk by spreading exposure across different asset classes.

TYPES OF BONDS

Bonds are like letting someone borrow your money, and they promise to pay it back with a little extra. There are different kinds of bonds, and here's how to explain them to a four-year-old:

1. Government Bonds

Imagine your mom or dad borrows your toy and promises to give it back with a sticker as a thank-you.

Government bonds are when the country (like the USA) borrows money from people and gives them extra back later. These are safe because the country always tries to pay back.

2. Municipal Bonds

This is like letting your town or city borrow your toy to build a new park or school.

They give your toy back later with a small reward, like a balloon.

3. Corporate Bonds

Imagine a big company, like the one that makes your favorite toys, needs to borrow money to make more toys.

They promise to give the money back with an extra treat, like a candy.

4. Junk Bonds

These are like letting a new kid at school borrow your toy, but you're not sure if they'll give it back.

They promise a big reward, but it's a little risky because you don't know them well.

TYPES OF BONDS

5. Savings Bonds

This is like giving money to your grandparents, and they keep it safe for you.

When you're older, they give it back with extra because they saved it for a long time.

6. Treasury Bonds

These are special bonds from the U.S. government that last a really long time, like 20 or 30 years.

It's like planting a tree and waiting for it to grow big and strong before you enjoy the fruit.

7. Convertible Bonds

Imagine you lend your toy to someone, and later, instead of getting it back, they give you something even cooler, like a shiny new toy.

That's like a bond that can turn into a stock if you want.

Bonds are different ways of lending your money to people or companies, and each type has its own rules for how they say thank you and when they pay you back!

PICKING BONDS

Picking bonds is like lending your toys to a friend who promises to give them back later, plus a little extra as a "thank you." Here's how it works:

The Borrower: Think of a bond as a piece of paper where a company or a city asks to borrow your money. They promise to give it back after a while.

The Thank You Gift: While they keep your money, they give you a little extra (grown-ups call it "interest") as a way to say thanks for helping.

Choose Who to Help: You pick someone you trust–like a company or city you think will keep their promise to give your money back.

Wait Patiently: You just sit and wait. When the time is up, they return your money, plus the thank-you gift!

It's like sharing your toy with someone who says, "I'll play with it carefully and give you a treat when I give it back!"

PICKING U. S. SAVINGS BONDS

Picking U.S. savings bonds is like giving your money to the government for safekeeping, and they promise to give it back with a little extra as a "thank you." Here's how it works:

Helping the Country: You're letting the country borrow your money, like sharing your toys with someone you trust a lot.

Growing Your Money: Over time, the money gets bigger, like planting a tiny seed and watching it grow into a tree with fruit.

Safe and Secure: It's super safe because it's like giving your money to the biggest and most trustworthy helper—the government!

A Long Wait: You have to wait a while to get your money back, but when it's time, they'll return it with extra money as a thank-you gift.

It's like saying, "Here's my toy—you can borrow it for a long time, but when you give it back, bring me some candy too!"

BASIC SIMPLE INVESTMENT ADVICE #3 that I heard but I didn't act on.

Many years ago, my dad told me that when he started working on a full-time job, that an older person told him to sign up for U.S. Savings Bonds and fill out the payroll deduction form for a $25.00 bond. So actually, he had $12.50 every two weeks deducted from his paycheck to purchase a bond that had an actual face value of $25.00. You are supposed to hold the bond at least 20 years to get the full value of the bond plus interest. The bonds stop earning interest after 30 years. He said the bonds were mailed to him and he had so many of them that he had to put them in a suitcase and he actually forgot about them. Later, as he started earning more money, he started buying $50 and $100 bonds.

When he was ready to make a major decision about a car after an old car broke down, he went to the bank and cashed in his old bonds He was able to buy a car outright with no monthly car payments!

PICKING U. S. TREASURY BONDS

Picking U.S. Treasury bonds is like giving your money to the country so they can take care of important things, and they promise to give it back with a little extra. Here's how it works:

Trusting a Big Helper: The country (called the government) is like a super big, strong friend you can trust to borrow your money and keep it safe.

Extra Thank You: When the country gives your money back, they say "thank you" by giving you a little extra money, like getting a treat for waiting.

Long Wait, Big Reward: You have to wait a long time, like waiting for your birthday. But when the wait is over, you get back what you gave, plus the extra.

Very Safe: It's super safe because the country always keeps its promises.

It's like letting the grown-ups borrow your toy, and they give it back with a cool sticker or candy as a thank-you gift!

PICKING U.S. TREASURY BILLS

Picking Treasury bills (T-bills) is like lending your money to the government for a short time and getting it back with a little extra. Here's how it works:

Short-Time Lending: It's like saying, "You can borrow my toy for just a little while, but don't forget to give it back soon!"

Small Thank-You Gift: When the government gives your money back, they say "thanks" by giving you a little extra money, like getting a small treat for sharing.

Very Safe: It's super safe because the government is like the most trustworthy friend who always keeps promises.

Quick Reward: You don't have to wait a long time, so it's great if you want your money back soon.

It's like sharing your favorite crayon for a week and getting it back with a fun sticker as a thank-you!

BASIC SIMPLE INVESTMENT ADVICE
#4 that I heard but
I didn't act on.

Many years ago, when I was around 22 years old, I used to work as a bank teller. There was a young male customer who would frequent the bank and get his passbook updated. He had a balance of over $100,000.00. I saw an initial deposit of $10,000.00 and then multiple deposits of $1,000.00I knew that he worked in a hospital, and he used to hand out visitor's passes. One day I decided to ask him how he got so much money. He smiled and he told me that when he graduated from college, instead of getting an old car as a present, his family gave him $10,000.00. Instead of him spending recklessly and blowing the money, he decided to invest in a $10,000 U.S. Treasury Bill. or Bond or Note. The interest was $1,000.00. Instead of spending the money, he bought another one and kept reinvesting and rolling over the CD (Certificate of Deposit) when it matured. I think he said. when he started working and earned $1,000.00, he kept investing and adding it to his account when the cd matures He kept buying, investing, and reinvesting the money. He said when he finds the right girl and gets married, he will have enough money to buy a house upfront! He was 26 years old, and I think the last time I had updated his passbook account, he had $126,000.00.

PASSBOOK AND CD EXPLANATION

Passbook Account

A passbook account is like having a piggy bank at a bank!

Put Money In: You can put your money in whenever you want, just like dropping coins into your piggy bank.

Take Money Out: If you need your money, you can take it out anytime, like opening your piggy bank to grab a coin for candy.

Safe and Growing: The bank keeps your money safe and gives you a tiny bit extra (called "interest") for saving it there.

A Book for Tracking: You get a little book (or an app) that shows how much money you've saved.

CD Account (Certificate of Deposit)

A CD account is like locking your money in a treasure chest for a while.

Lock It Up: You give your money to the bank and agree not to touch it for a certain amount of time, like a year or more.

More Extra Money: Because you're patient and leave it locked, the bank gives you more "thank-you money" (interest) than with a passbook account.

Wait Patiently: You can't take the money out early without a penalty, so you have to wait until the time is up, like waiting for your birthday to open a gift.

Bigger Reward: When the time is up, you get all your money back, plus a bigger extra gift from the bank!

The Difference:

Passbook Account: You can put in or take out money whenever you want, but the bank gives you a small thank-you.

CD Account: You have to wait a long time to get your money back, but the thank-you gift is much bigger!

It's like choosing between using your piggy bank now or locking up a treasure chest to open later with more goodies inside!

TO-DO LIST

#1	
#2	
#3	
#4	
#5	

TO-DO LIST

#6	
#7	
#8	
#9	
#10	

NOTES

TOPIC ______________________ DATE ______________

NOTES

ACTION ITEMS

- [ ]
- [ ]
- [ ]
- [ ]
- [ ]

Mutual Funds

7. Professional Management

Mutual funds are managed by professional fund managers who make decisions on buying and selling securities. This expertise can be beneficial for investors who prefer a hands-off approach.

8. Diversification

Mutual funds pool money from many investors to buy a diversified portfolio of stocks, bonds, or other securities, reducing risk through diversification.

9. Accessibility

Mutual funds are accessible to investors with smaller amounts of capital, providing an opportunity to invest in a broad range of assets without needing to purchase them individually.

TYPES OF MUTUAL FUNDS

Mutual funds are like a group of people putting their money together to buy cool stuff, and a grown-up called a "manager" decides what to buy. There are different types of mutual funds, and here's how to explain them to a four-year-old:

1. Stock Mutual Funds

Imagine you and your friends all put your money together to buy little pieces of big companies, like your favorite toy company.

The goal is to share the money you get if the companies do really well and grow.

2. Bond Mutual Funds

This is like everyone in the group lending money to companies or cities. They pay back the money with extra, and everyone in the group shares the reward.

3. Money Market Funds

These are like putting your money in a super-safe piggy bank.

It doesn't grow a lot, but it's always there when you need it.

4. Index Funds

Imagine you're collecting every color of crayon in the box without picking them one by one.

An index fund buys a little bit of everything from a list of companies, so it's easy and simple.

TYPES OF MUTUAL FUNDS

5. Balanced Funds

This is like having a lunchbox with a mix of healthy snacks and a little treat.

It has both stocks (for growing money) and bonds (for keeping it safe).

6. Sector Funds

Imagine a fund that only buys things from one area, like toys, cars, or yummy food.

It focuses on just one type of business, like only toy companies.

7. International Funds

This is like using your money to buy stuff from other countries, like a cool toy from Japan or a sweet treat from France.

It's fun because you get to explore the world with your money!

8. Target-Date Funds

Imagine you're saving for a big party on your 18th birthday.

This fund plans ahead, starting with risky things (to grow money fast) and then safer things as the party gets closer.

9. Dividend Funds

These funds buy stocks that share candy (money) regularly.

It's like getting a treat every month or so without waiting too long.

Mutual funds are like team projects where everyone shares the money they make, and each type is a different way to play the money game!

PICKING MUTUAL FUNDS

Picking mutual funds is like joining a group of friends to buy a big bag of toys that everyone shares. Here's how it works:

Teamwork: You and your friends each put in some money to buy a big bag of toys. The money adds up so you can get lots of different toys together.

Many Kinds of Toys: Inside the bag, there are cars, dolls, blocks, and all kinds of fun things. A mutual fund has lots of companies or investments all in one.

A Helper to Pick: There's a grown-up (called a fund manager) who helps pick the best toys for the bag. They do all the hard work, so you don't have to choose on your own.

Sharing the Fun: When the toys in the bag become more valuable, everyone gets their share of the extra money. It's like sharing the treasure when your group finds something really cool.

It's like saying, "Let's all work together, get the best toys, and share the fun and rewards!"

TO-DO LIST

#1	
#2	
#3	
#4	
#5	

TO-DO LIST

#6	
#7	
#8	
#9	
#10	

NOTES

TOPIC ______________________ DATE ____________

NOTES

ACTION ITEMS

- [ ]
- [ ]
- [ ]
- [ ]
- [ ]

DRIP'S

DIVIDENT REINVESTMENT PLANS

4. DRIPs (Dividend Reinvestment Plans)

DRIPs are like getting candy for sharing, and then using that candy to get even more candy. If your pizza slice earns you more pizza bites, and instead of eating them, you use them to buy more slices, that's a DRIP. You're reinvesting what you earn.

Dividend Reinvestment Plans (DRIPs)

10. Compounding Returns

DRIPs allow investors to reinvest dividends to purchase more shares, leading to compounding returns over time. This reinvestment can significantly increase the growth potential of your investments.

11. Cost Efficiency

DRIPs often allow you to purchase additional shares without paying transaction fees, making it a cost-effective way to increase your investment.

12. Dollar-Cost Averaging

By regularly reinvesting dividends, you benefit from dollar-cost averaging, reducing the impact of market volatility on your investment.

DRIP'S DIVIDEND REINVESTMENT PLANS

DRIPs, or Dividend Reinvestment Plans, are like growing your candy stash by using the candy you already have! When companies give you treats (dividends), you can use them to get even more pieces of the company instead of just eating the candy. Let's explain the different types of DRIPs to a four-year-old:

1. Company-Sponsored DRIPs

Imagine a toy company gives you candy every time they sell toys. Instead of eating the candy, you use it to get more toys from the company.

Some companies let you do this directly with them, and they might even give you a little extra for joining!

2. Broker-Sponsored DRIPs

This is like asking a grown-up (a broker) to help you use your candy to get more toys from different companies.

The broker helps you handle everything in one place, so you don't have to talk to each toy company.

3. No-Fee DRIPs

These are the best because they don't charge you anything extra when you use your candy to get more toys.

It's like trading candy without anyone taking a piece for themselves!

DRIP'S
DIVIDEND REINVESTMENT PLANS

4. Discount DRIPs

Some companies say, "If you use your candy to buy more toys, we'll give you a discount!"

It's like getting a new toy for fewer pieces of candy than usual.

5. Optional Cash Purchase DRIPs

In this type, you can add extra allowance (money) to buy even more toys from the company.

It's like putting your pocket money and candy together to get bigger or better toys.

6. Partial DRIPs

You don't have to use all your candy to get new toys; you can save some for later and still grow your stash.

It's like sharing only a few candies to get a new toy while keeping the rest for yourself.

7. Tax-Advantaged DRIPs

This type helps you save more because you don't have to give away as much of your candy to the "Candy Tax Collector."

It's like keeping more candy for yourself while still growing your stash.

DRIPs are a fun way to grow your collection without spending extra money–just by using the treats companies give you!

PICKING DRIP'S

Picking DRIPs (Dividend Reinvestment Plans) is like getting treats that can grow into even more treats! Here's how it works, in a simple way:

Getting Treats (Dividends): Imagine you own a little piece of a candy shop. Every time the shop does well, it gives you a few candies as a thank-you.

Saving the Treats: Instead of eating the candies, you put them back into the shop to help it grow even bigger.

More Treats Over Time: As the shop grows bigger, it can give you even more candies next time. It's like a magic candy machine that makes more and more candies the longer you wait.

Easy to Do: DRIPs let you keep growing your candy stash without needing to do much–just sit back and watch it grow!

It's like saving some of your Halloween candy so you can trade it later for even more candy!

TO-DO LIST

#1	
#2	
#3	
#4	
#5	

TO-DO LIST

#6	
#7	
#8	
#9	
#10	

NOTES

TOPIC ____________________ **DATE** ____________

NOTES

ACTION ITEMS

- [ ]
- [ ]
- [ ]
- [ ]
- [ ]

REIT'S
REAL ESTATE
INVESTMENT TRUSTS

5. REITs (Real Estate Investment Trusts)

REITs are like owning part of a big playground or house without buying it all.

Imagine you and your friends each pay a little money to help build a playground. Now, everyone owns a tiny piece and gets to share in the fun (or the rent money if it's a house).

Real Estate Investment Trusts (REITs)

13. Real Estate Exposure

REITs provide exposure to the real estate market without the need to directly purchase or manage properties. This allows investors to benefit from real estate appreciation and income.

14. Regular Income

REITs typically pay high dividends as they are required to distribute a significant portion of their income to shareholders, providing a steady income stream.

15. Portfolio Diversification

Adding REITs to your portfolio diversifies your investments across different sectors, reducing risk and enhancing potential returns.

In conclusion, investing in stocks, bonds, mutual funds, DRIPs, and REITs offers a range of benefits that can help you achieve financial growth, income generation, and risk diversification. By understanding the unique advantages of each investment type, you can build a well-rounded portfolio that aligns with your financial goals and risks.

REIT'S REAL ESTATE INVESTMENT TRUSTS

REITs (Real Estate Investment Trusts) are like piggy banks that hold money to buy buildings and places where people live, work, or shop. Here's how to explain the types of REITs to a four-year-old:

1. Residential REITs

These are like big apartment buildings or houses where people live.

The REIT makes money when people pay rent to stay there, like sharing your toys for a fee.

2. Commercial REITs

These own places where people work, like offices or stores.

It's like renting out a playroom for other kids to use for their games.

3. Retail REITs

These own shopping malls and stores where people buy toys, clothes, and snacks.

Every time someone shops there, the REIT makes money, like having a lemonade stand in your yard.

4. Industrial REITs

These own big warehouses where toys and goods are stored before they go to stores.

It's like keeping all your blocks in a giant toy chest for others to borrow.

5. Healthcare REITs

These own hospitals, nursing homes, and medical offices.

It's like helping doctors and nurses by giving them a place to work, and they pay rent to the REIT.

PICKING REITS
REAL ESTATE INVESTMENT TRUSTS

Picking REITs (Real Estate Investment Trusts) is like helping to own big buildings and getting a share of the money they make. Here's how it works for a four-year-old:

Owning Big Buildings Together: Imagine you and a bunch of people put your money together to "own" things like malls, apartments, or office buildings. You don't own the whole thing, just a little piece.

Earning Rent Money: The people who live or work in these buildings pay rent, and you get a share of that rent as money back. It's like letting your friend play with your toys, and they give you a snack for it.

Growing Money: If the buildings become more popular or worth more money, your share grows bigger too, like planting a tree and watching it grow tall.

Easy Ownership: You don't have to take care of the buildings yourself. Other people handle that part, so it's super easy!

It's like sharing a pretend castle with your friends and getting fun rewards whenever someone plays there!

TO-DO LIST

#1	
#2	
#3	
#4	
#5	

TO-DO LIST

#6	
#7	
#8	
#9	
#10	

NOTES

TOPIC ____________________ **DATE** ____________

NOTES

ACTION ITEMS

- [ ]
- [ ]
- [ ]
- [ ]
- [ ]

ETF'S EXCHANGE TRADED FUNDS

6. ETFs (Exchange-Traded Funds)
ETFs are like a grab bag of toys that you can trade with others.
It's like buying a bag filled with different toys (stocks, bonds, etc.) at the store. You can trade the bag with friends anytime.

What Are ETF'S?

Imagine ETFs as a big toy box filled with lots of different toys, like blocks, cars, and dolls. Here's how they work, just like when you play with your toys:

A Big Toy Box

ETFs are like a big toy box that holds many different kinds of toys inside. Instead of just having one toy, you have a whole collection to play with. This means you can enjoy many different toys at the same time!

Lots of Choices

Just like you can have blocks, cars, and dolls in your toy box, ETFs have different things inside, like pretend pieces of companies, pretend money, or even pretend gold. This makes playing with your toy box super exciting because there's always something new to discover!

Easy to Share

ETFs are like a toy box that you can share with your friends. You can open it up and show them all the cool toys you have inside. You can even trade toys with your friends during playtime, just like buying and selling ETFs.

Safe and Fun

Having all these toys in one big box makes it safe and fun because you won't lose them easily. Plus, if you ever get bored with one toy, there are plenty of others to play with, just like how ETFs keep things interesting by having lots of different things inside.

So, think of ETFs as a special toy box that lets you have lots of fun with many different toys all at once. Isn't that a neat way to think about it?

ETF'S EXCHANGE TRADED FUNDS

ETFs, or Exchange-Traded Funds, are like baskets full of goodies you can buy and sell at a store. Each basket has different things inside, and here's how to explain the types of ETFs to a four-year-old:

1. Stock ETFs

Imagine a basket full of tiny pieces of many companies, like toy makers, candy companies, or video game creators.

If these companies do well, your basket becomes more valuable!

2. Bond ETFs

This basket has lots of "IOUs" from companies or cities.

It's like lending out toys and getting them back with stickers as a thank-you.

3. Commodity ETFs

This basket is filled with cool stuff from nature, like gold, oil, or even yummy things like coffee or sugar.

It's like collecting shiny rocks or sweet treats.

4. Sector ETFs

These baskets focus on just one type of thing, like all the toy makers or all the car builders.

It's like having a basket filled with only your favorite toy brands.

5. International ETFs

This basket is filled with things from all around the world, like a soccer ball from Brazil or chocolates from Switzerland.

It's like exploring different countries with your money.

ETFs are like shopping for baskets with different cool things inside, and you pick the one that matches what you like or need!

ETF'S EXCHANGE TRADED FUNDS

6. Dividend ETFs

This basket collects stocks that share candy (money) regularly with you.

It's like having a basket that gives you treats every few weeks.

7. Growth ETFs

This basket is filled with fast-growing companies, like planting seeds that could turn into big trees.

It's exciting because the basket might grow bigger quickly!

8. Value ETFs

These baskets have companies that are like hidden treasures—they might not look shiny now but could become super valuable later.

It's like finding a plain rock that turns out to be a diamond.

9. Thematic ETFs

This is a fun basket focused on one big idea, like robots, green energy, or space travel.

It's like filling your basket with only futuristic toys and gadgets.

10. Index ETFs

These baskets hold a little bit of everything from a big list of companies, like crayons in every color of the rainbow.

It's simple and covers a lot!

PICKING ETF'S
EXCHANGE-TRADED FUNDS

Picking ETFs (Exchange-Traded Funds) is like getting a big box of toys where each toy is different, but they all come together in one set.

Here's how it works:

A Box of Many Things: An ETF is like a toy box that has lots of different toys inside, like cars, dolls, and blocks. With an ETF, you get to own small pieces of many companies all at once.

Easy to Share: You can trade your ETF toy box with others anytime you want, just like swapping toys with friends at a playdate.

Safer and Fun: Because you have many toys (or companies) in one box, if one toy isn't fun anymore, you still have lots of others to play with. This makes it safer and more exciting!

Affordable: Instead of buying lots of different toys one by one, you get them all in one box, which is easier and sometimes cheaper.

It's like saying, "I want to play with a little bit of everything, so I'll pick the big toy box that has it all!"

TO-DO LIST

#1	
#2	
#3	
#4	
#5	

TO-DO LIST

#6	
#7	
#8	
#9	
#10	

NOTES

TOPIC ______________________ DATE ______________

NOTES

ACTION ITEMS

COMMODITIES

COMMODITIES

7. Commodities

Commodities are things we all use, like food or metal.

If you collect shiny rocks or bananas and trade them with others, that's like commodities.

They're basic things people buy and sell, like gold, oil, or crops.

These are all different ways grown-ups save, share, and grow their money, like turning small ideas into big adventures!

WHAT ARE COMMODITIES?

Commodities are things we use every day that come from nature or farms. Here's a simple way to explain:

Basic Stuff Everyone Needs:

Commodities are like the building blocks of the world—things like food, shiny metals, or fuel for cars. Imagine things like bananas, rice, gold, or even the stuff that makes crayons.

People Buy and Sell Them:

Grown-ups buy and sell these things to help make or grow other things. For example, a baker buys flour (a commodity) to bake bread.

Comes from Nature:

Many commodities come from the earth or farms, like wheat from a field or oil from deep underground. It's like finding treasure in nature.

Trading:

People can trade commodities, like swapping bananas for apples or shiny rocks for candy. It's how they share things they need.

So, commodities are the everyday stuff that people use to make life work, just like how crayons and paper help you draw fun pictures!

HARD COMMODITIES

Commodities are usually grouped into two main types: hard commodities and soft commodities. Here's a list of the different types:

I. Hard Commodities

These are natural resources that are mined or extracted from the earth:

Energy

Oil (Crude Oil, Brent Oil, WTI)

Natural Gas

Coal

Electricity

Metals

Gold

Silver

Platinum

Copper

Aluminum

Steel

SOFT COMMODITIES

2. Soft Commodities

These are agricultural products or livestock that are grown or raised:

Grains

Wheat

Corn

Rice

Oats

Barley

Oilseeds

Soybeans

Canola

Sunflower Seeds

Livestock and Meat

Cattle (Live Cattle, Feeder Cattle)

Pork (Lean Hogs)

Dairy

Milk

Cheese

Butter

Other Agriculture

Sugar

Coffee

Cocoa (used to make chocolate)

Cotton

PICKING COMMODITIES

Picking commodities is like choosing to play with stuff that comes from nature or is used to make things we need. Here's how it works:

What Are Commodities? They're things like gold, oil, wheat, or even oranges. Think of them as the building blocks for stuff we use every day, like food, toys, or cars.

Buying the Stuff: Grown-ups can buy a little piece of these things, like owning some gold or a bunch of wheat. It's like picking your favorite thing to collect, like shiny rocks or cool shells.

Value Goes Up and Down: The value of commodities can change, like how lemonade is more fun to sell on a hot day than a cold day. Grown-ups try to guess when their value will go up to make more money.

Helps Everyone: Commodities are important because people all over the world need them, like bread for sandwiches or fuel for cars.

It's like saying, "I want to pick something super useful, like apples or shiny gold, and see how much it's worth later!"

ADDITIONAL CATEGORIES

ADDITIONAL CATEGORIES

3. Additional Categories

Precious Stones: Diamonds (sometimes considered a commodity in markets)

Forestry Products: Lumber (used for building)

These commodities are essential to the global economy, as they are the raw materials for most of the things we use and consume every day!

PRECIOUS STONES

Precious stones sold as commodities are like super special shiny rocks that people think are very valuable. Here's how to explain it to a four-year-old:

What Are Precious Stones?

Precious stones are sparkly rocks, like diamonds, rubies, emeralds, and sapphires. They're really pretty, and people use them to make jewelry like rings, necklaces, and crowns.

Why Are They Special?

These stones are rare, which means you can't find them everywhere. It's like looking for a shiny treasure in a big sandbox—you don't find it often, so it's really exciting when you do.

Buying and Selling Them

Grown-ups buy and sell these shiny stones, kind of like trading toys. They do this because the stones are valuable and can be used to make beautiful things or saved like treasure.

Used All Over the World

People in different countries love these stones because they're shiny, rare, and last forever. It's like a shiny rock collection that everyone wants to have.

So, precious stones sold as commodities are like the ultimate treasure hunt—people find them, trade them, and use them to make beautiful and special things!

FORESTRY PRODUCTS

Forestry products sold as commodities are things made from trees that people use every day. Here's how to explain it to a four-year-old:

What Are Forestry Products?

Forestry products are all the cool things we can make from trees! It's like turning tree trunks and branches into stuff we use, like paper, pencils, or wooden blocks.

Why Are They Important?

Trees give us wood for building houses, making furniture, and even toys. They also help make paper for coloring books and magazines. Trees are like nature's gift that keeps giving.

Buying and Selling Wood

Grown-ups trade big logs or wood pieces (called lumber) to help build things like schools, playgrounds, or fences. It's like sharing building blocks with friends to make something amazing.

From Forests to the World

People take care of forests so we can keep using trees for important things. They grow new trees after cutting some down, just like planting seeds in a garden to grow more plants.

So, forestry products are the useful things we get from trees, and grown-ups sell and trade them so we can have what we need to build, write, and play!

TO-DO LIST

#1	
#2	
#3	
#4	
#5	

TO-DO LIST

#6	
#7	
#8	
#9	
#10	

NOTES

TOPIC ______________________ **DATE** ____________

NOTES

ACTION ITEMS

EXTRAS

THE IMPORTANCE OF SAVING FOR RETIREMENT

Imagine you have a giant toy chest.

Right now, every time you get a toy, you put one inside the chest instead of playing with it. At first, it looks like you have fewer toys to play with, but guess what? This is a magic toy chest!

Over time, the chest gives you extra toys for every toy you save! The more toys you put in early, the more it gives you later.

One day, when you get older and don't get as many new toys anymore, you can open the chest and—WOW!—you have so many toys waiting for you!

That's what saving for retirement is like. You put money away when you're younger so that when you're older and not working as much, you still have lots of money to enjoy life!

SAVINGS ACCOUNT OR AN INVESTMENT ACCOUNT?

Imagine you have two trees you can plant.

Saving Account - The Slow & Steady Tree

This tree grows very slowly but never stops growing. Every year, it adds a tiny new branch. Over time, it gets a little bigger, but it takes a long time to grow into a big tree. This is like a savings account—your money grows safely but slowly with interest.

Investment Account - The Fast & Wild Tree

This tree grows much faster, and some years, it sprouts lots of fruit and branches! But sometimes, the wind shakes it, and a few branches fall off. Even though it goes up and down, over time, it still grows much bigger than the slow tree. This is like an investment account—your money can grow much faster, but sometimes it can go up and down before it gets big.

Which One Is Better?

If you want safe and steady growth, the savings account is great. But if you want your tree to grow much bigger over time, even with a few bumps along the way, an investment account can help your money grow more!

INVESTING IN THE STOCK MARKET

Imagine you have a lemonade stand.
At first, you have just one stand. But what if you help a friend start their own stand too? In return, they share some of their money with you when they make sales.
Now, imagine you help lots of friends start lemonade stands all over town. The more stands there are, the more money you get over time–without having to sell all the lemonade yourself!
That's like investing in the stock market! Instead of working for all your money, you help big companies grow by investing, and in return, they share their success with you. The longer you wait, the more your money can grow and grow!

EARNING INTEREST ON A SAVINGS ACCOUNT

Imagine you have a cookie jar. Every time you put a cookie in, a magic fairy comes at night and adds a tiny piece of a cookie as a reward. If you keep your cookies in the jar, the fairy keeps adding more and more little pieces.

But if you eat the cookies too soon, the fairy won't have as many cookies to grow!

This is just like a savings account–if you leave your money there, it grows by itself because the bank gives you extra money (called interest). And over time, the extra money also earns more extra money! That's called compounding interest–it's like your cookies making more cookies!

So, the longer you save and wait, the more cookies (or money!) you'll have in the future!

SIMPLE INTEREST AND COMPOUND INTERST

Imagine you let your friend borrow one of your toy cars. They promise to give it back in a few days plus one extra sticker as a "thank you" for borrowing it.

Next time, if you let them borrow another car, they only give you one more sticker again–not more than last time. That's how simple interest works! The bank gives you extra money for saving, but it's always the same amount each time, based only on what you first put in. It doesn't grow bigger like magic.

But if you want your stickers (or money) to grow faster, you might want compounding interest instead–because that's like stickers earning more stickers!

COMPOUNDING INTEREST

Imagine you have a gumball machine.
Every time you put a gumball inside, a magic fairy adds an extra gumball as a reward.
The next time, the fairy not only gives you a gumball for what you put in, but also for the extra gumballs she gave you before! So, your gumball pile keeps growing faster and faster without you doing anything!
That's how compounding interest works! The more you save, the more your money grows over time—because your extra money also starts earning more money!

COMPOUNDING INTEREST FOR A SAVINGS AND AN INVESTMENT ACCOUNT

Imagine you have a magic piggy bank.

For a Savings Account:

Every time you put money in, the piggy bank gives you a little extra as a "thank you" for saving. If you leave your money there, next time the piggy bank gives you even more, because now it's giving extra on both the money you put in and the extra it gave you before! Over time, your money grows bigger and bigger without you doing anything!

For an Investment Portfolio:

Now, imagine you plant a tiny apple seed. At first, it's just a little sprout. But if you wait and take care of it, it grows into a tree with apples. You can sell some apples and buy more seeds, planting even more trees. The more trees you have, the more apples grow! Over time, your apple farm keeps getting bigger and bigger, just like your money when you invest it wisely.

So, saving is like a magic piggy bank giving you extra money, and investing is like growing an apple farm that keeps making more apples. The longer you wait, the bigger your money (or apples) will grow!

CAN I DOUBLE MY MONEY?
WHAT IS THE RULE OF 72?

Imagine you have a magic doubling machine for your money. The Rule of 72 is a special trick that helps you figure out how long it will take for your money to double!

Here's how it works:

Take the number 72 and divide it by the "growing speed" (interest rate) of your money.

The answer tells you how many years it will take for your money to double!

For example:

If your money grows at 3% per year, you do 72 ÷ 3 = 24 years to double.

If your money grows at 5% per year, you do 72 ÷ 5 = 14.4 years to double.

If your money grows at 6% per year, you do 72 ÷ 6 = 12 years to double.

If your money grows 8% per year, you do 72 ÷ 8 = 9 years to double!

If your money grows 9% per year, you do 72 ÷ 9 = 8 years to double!

If your money grows 12% per year, you do 72 ÷ 12 =6 years to double!

So, the faster the money grows, the sooner it doubles like magic!

It's like if you planted one apple tree, and every few years, the tree magically grew another tree. The faster the magic works, the sooner you have a whole orchard!

WILL THE SAVINGS ACCOUNT MAKE YOU RICHER?

Imagine you have a piggy bank that gives you a tiny coin every year as a "thank you" for saving.
If you put your money in there and leave it for a long time, you'll get more coins, but just a few each year. Over many, many years, you'll have a little more, but it won't make you super rich because the piggy bank gives only a tiny bit of extra money.
Getting rich means you need your money to grow much faster than that. So, while a savings account is safe and helps you grow your money a little, to get really rich, you need to find ways that help your money grow faster, like investing in things that can grow big!

WILL THE INVESTMENT ACCOUNT MAKE YOUR RICHER?

Imagine you plant a magic apple tree in your backyard. At first, it grows slowly, but over time, it starts growing more and more apples each year! Some years, the apples might fall off or get a little squished, but after a long time, the tree has lots and lots of apples!

Now, an investment account is like that magic apple tree! Your money can grow faster than in a savings account, because it can earn more money over time, just like the apples growing on the tree. But sometimes, the tree might lose a few apples, and other times, it gets really big and strong!

So, if you leave your money in an investment account for a long time, it can grow really big and help you get rich– but it's important to remember, sometimes it can grow slower or lose a little before it gets huge!

SHORT TERM GOALS
AND
LONG TERM GOALS

Imagine you want to buy two things.

Short-Term Goal - The Toy You Want Right Now

This is like when you want a new toy–something you can get soon! You save a little bit of money every day, and in a short time, you have enough to buy it!

Long-Term Goal - The Big Dream House or Vacation

This is like wanting to buy a big house or go on a special vacation one day when you're much older. It takes a long time to save up all the money for something really big!

So, short-term goals are for things you want now, like a toy, and long-term goals are for things you want much later, like a big house or a fun trip. You have to be patient and save little by little for the long-term goals!

THE IMPORTANCE OF HAVING MULTIPLE STREAMS OF INCOME

Imagine you have an ice cream cart.

Every day, you sell ice cream and make money. But what if it rains one day and no one buys ice cream? Uh-oh! No money that day!

Now, imagine you also have a lemonade stand and a cookie shop. If it rains and no one buys ice cream, people might still buy cookies and lemonade!

Having multiple streams of income means you don't have to worry if one way of making money slows down—because you have other ways to keep getting money!

Just like having different snacks to sell, having different ways to make money helps you stay safe and grow your savings!

HOW TO ESTABLISH BUILDING WEALTH GOALS

Imagine you want to build the biggest and best toy collection ever!

To do that, you need a plan! Here's how:

1. Decide What You Want

First, think about what you want in the future. Do you want a big house? A fast car? Lots of money to buy toys?

2. Figure Out How Much You Need

If a toy costs 10 coins, you need to save 10 coins. If a big house costs 1,000 coins, you need to save much more!

3. Make a Plan to Get There

You can:

Save some of your allowance in a piggy bank.

Invest some money so it grows bigger over time.

Find new ways to make money, like selling lemonade!

4. Be Patient and Keep Going!

Wealth doesn't grow overnight! But if you keep saving, investing, and making smart choices, one day you'll have everything you dreamed of!

So, building wealth is like collecting toys—you start small, keep adding more, and one day, you'll have a huge collection!

NOTES

TOPIC ______________________ **DATE** ____________

NOTES

ACTION ITEMS

- [ ]
- [ ]
- [ ]
- [ ]
- [ ]

Whether you are just starting out or starting over, I hope that this book helps you move one step a day towards your financial freedom journey.

*DISCLAIMER: I AM NOT A PROFESSIONAL. THIS IS FOR EDUCATIONAL/INFORMATIONAL PURPOSES ONLY. THIS IS A SIMPLE BASIC GUIDE TO GETTING STARTED OR STARTING OVER.

INVEST AT YOUR OWN RISK.

TO-DO LIST

#1	
#2	
#3	
#4	
#5	

TO-DO LIST

#6	
#7	
#8	
#9	
#10	

NOTES

TOPIC ____________ DATE ____________

NOTES

ACTION ITEMS

- [ ]
- [ ]
- [ ]
- [ ]
- [ ]

www.ingramcontent.com/pod-product-compliance
Lightning Source LLC
LaVergne TN
LVHW082246150826
845677LV00009B/1542

* 9 7 9 8 9 8 9 4 3 7 0 7 8 *